MY FIRST LOOK AT PETS

Hamsters are cute and playful pets

Hamsters

VALERIE BODDEN

CREATIVE EDUCATION

Published by Creative Education

123 South Broad Street, Mankato, Minnesota 56001

Creative Education is an imprint of The Creative Company

Designed by Rita Marshall

Photographs by Alamy (Renee Morris, Papilio, Profimedia.CZ.s.r.o., Maximiliam Weinzierl),

Getty Images (GK Hart / Vikki Hart, Mahaux Photography, MUSTAFA OZER / AFP,

Photodisc Collection)

Copyright © 2007 Creative Education

Printed in the United States of America

Library of Congress Cataloging-in-Publication Data

Bodden, Valerie. Hamsters / by Valerie Bodden.

p. cm. — (My first look at pets)

Includes bibliographical references and index.

ISBN-13 : 978-1-58341-459-0

1. Hamsters as pets—Juvenile literature. 1. Title. 11. Series.

SF459.H3.B63 2005   636.935'6—dc22   2005050696

First edition 9 8 7 6 5 4 3 2 1

HAMSTERS

SMALL AND FURRY

At first glance, hamsters look like mice. Hamsters are related to mice. But hamsters have shorter tails than mice. Hamsters are bigger, too.

Hamsters are **rodents**. They have round bodies and soft fur. They have small ears. Hamsters have pouches in their cheeks to hold food. They have big **incisor teeth** that are always growing. They need to chew on wood to wear their teeth down.

THIS HAMSTER'S CHEEK POUCHES ARE FULL

Hamsters have a very good sense of smell. They can hear well, too. But they cannot see very well. Hamsters usually do not make any sounds.

Choosing a Hamster

There are many different kinds of hamsters. Some live only in the wild. Others make good pets.

Some hamsters can
figure out how to open
their cage and escape!

HAMSTERS ARE VERY CURIOUS ANIMALS

Golden hamsters are the most common kind of pet hamsters. They are the best hamsters for kids. Golden hamsters are about the size of a chipmunk. They are also called Syrian hamsters.

Russian hamsters and Chinese hamsters also make good pets. They are both smaller than golden hamsters.

Hamsters can run up to

eight miles (13 km) a night

on an exercise wheel!

Male hamsters usually make better pets than females. They do not get as cranky. Most pet hamsters live two to three years. But some can live up to four years.

HAMSTER CARE

Hamsters need to be kept in a cage. Golden hamsters do not like living with other hamsters. They each need their own cage. If two hamsters share a cage, they might fight. Other kinds of hamsters can live in **pairs** or small groups.

HAMSTERS LIVE FOR A FEW YEARS

Hamsters should have an exercise wheel in their cage. The floor of the cage should be covered with **wood shavings**. Hamsters also like some bedding in their cage. Pieces of paper towel make good bedding.

Hamsters need healthy hamster food. They need lots of fresh water, too. Hamsters do not need baths. But hamsters with very long fur should be brushed with a toothbrush.

WOOD SHAVINGS SHOULD BE REPLACED OFTEN

SOME HAMSTERS LIKE TO EAT NUTS

Hamster Fun

Hamsters are **nocturnal** animals. They like to sleep during the day and be active at night. Hamsters like to spend time with their owners. Some hamsters like to be petted. Some like to be held.

Hamsters should be picked up with two hands. They should not be squeezed or held too tightly. Hamsters should not be lifted

Hawaii is an island.

It is against the law to

own a hamster there!

HAMSTERS LIKE TO CLIMB INTO THINGS

high off the ground. They might try to jump and could hurt themselves.

Hamsters love to play and are fun to watch. Hamsters like to play in toilet paper rolls. They like to play with toys they can chew on. Most of all, hamsters like to know that their owners love them!

A golden hamster can
carry up to half its body
weight in its cheek pouches.

BESIDES PLAYING, HAMSTERS LOVE TO EAT

Hands-on: Match the Smell

Hamsters have a great sense of smell. How good is your sense of smell? Try this activity to find out.

What You Need

Five film canisters with holes poked in the lids

A small piece of banana

A small piece of chocolate

Coffee grounds

A small clump of dirt

A cotton ball soaked in vinegar

What You Do

1. Place one item in each canister.
2. Put the lids on the canisters.
3. Mix up the canisters.
4. Smell the canisters and try to guess what is inside each. Then open the canisters to see if you were right.
5. Test your friends to see how well they do!

HAMSTERS USE THEIR NOSE TO FIND FOOD

Index

Words to Know

incisor teeth—sharp front teeth used for cutting food

nocturnal—active at night

pairs—groups of two

rodents—small, furry animals that chew a lot

wood shavings—small, thin pieces of wood

Read More

Hibbert, Clare. *Hamster*. North Mankato, Minn.: Smart Apple Media, 2005.

Nelson, Robin. *Pet Hamster*. Minneapolis: Lerner, 2003.

Ross, Veronica. *My First Hamster*. North Mankato, Minn.: Thameside Press, 2002.

Explore the Web

Enchanted Learning: Hamster http://www.allaboutnature.com/subjects/mammals/rodent/Hamsterprintout.shtml

Hamsters! Take the 10-Minute Bedtime Tour! http://www.hamstertours.com/index.html

Hamster Students http://www2.tltc.ttu.edu/thomas/classPet/1999/Hamster/student.htm